MATH
WORD
PROBLEMS

ADDITION

ADDITION

1. Jake has 7 pears and Brian has 9 pears. How many pears do Jake and Brian have together?

2. 3 apples were in the basket. More apples were added to the basket. Now there are 7 apples. How many apples were added to the basket?

3. 9 balls are in the basket. 10 more balls are put in the basket. How many balls are in the basket now?

4. Some peaches were in the basket. 5 more peaches were added to the basket. Now there are 15 peaches. How many peaches were in the basket before more peaches were added?

ADDITION

5. **2 pears were in the basket. More pears were added to the basket. Now there are 4 pears. How many pears were added to the basket?**

---

6. **6 red marbles and 9 green marbles are in the basket. How many marbles are in the basket?**

---

7. **15 balls were in the basket. 8 are red and the rest are green. How many balls are green?**

---

8. **Marcie has 7 more oranges than Marin. Marin has 8 oranges. How many oranges does Marcie have?**

ADDITION

9. **Allan has 10 peaches and Donald has 4 peaches. How many peaches do Allan and Donald have together?**

10. **3 plums are in the basket. 2 more plums are put in the basket. How many plums are in the basket now?**

11. **6 marbles were in the basket. 3 are red and the rest are green. How many marbles are green?**

12. **Some balls were in the basket. 7 more balls were added to the basket. Now there are 17 balls. How many balls were in the basket before more balls were added?**

ADDITION

13. Paul has 2 apples and Steven has 8 apples. How many apples do Paul and Steven have together?

----

14. Ellen has 2 more marbles than Sandra. Sandra has 8 marbles. How many marbles does Ellen have?

----

15. 14 bananas were in the basket. 10 are red and the rest are green. How many bananas are green?

----

16. 2 apricots were in the basket. More apricots were added to the basket. Now there are 4 apricots. How many apricots were added to the basket?

ADDITION

17. **5 plums are in the basket. 6 more plums are put in the basket. How many plums are in the basket now?**

18. **Michele has 2 more bananas than Sandra. Sandra has 6 bananas. How many bananas does Michele have?**

19. **7 pears were in the basket. 4 are red and the rest are green. How many pears are green?**

20. **4 red apricots and 8 green apricots are in the basket. How many apricots are in the basket?**

ADDITION

21. Some pears were in the basket. 9 more pears were added to the basket. Now there are 15 pears. How many pears were in the basket before more pears were added?

---

22. Marin has 13 more apricots than Sharon. Sharon has 12 apricots. How many apricots does Marin have?

---

23. Donald has 14 oranges and Adam has 6 oranges. How many oranges do Donald and Adam have together?

---

24. 14 balls were in the basket. 5 are red and the rest are green. How many balls are green?

ADDITION

25. **11 pears were in the basket. 6 are red and the rest are green. How many pears are green?**

26. **Donald has 14 balls and Paul has 12 balls. How many balls do Donald and Paul have together?**

27. **Some oranges were in the basket. 4 more oranges were added to the basket. Now there are 6 oranges. How many oranges were in the basket before more oranges were added?**

28. **15 plums are in the basket. 3 more plums are put in the basket. How many plums are in the basket now?**

ADDITION

29. 9 balls are in the basket. 11 more balls are put in the basket. How many balls are in the basket now?

30. 4 plums were in the basket. More plums were added to the basket. Now there are 15 plums. How many plums were added to the basket?

31. 17 apricots were in the basket. 3 are red and the rest are green. How many apricots are green?

32. Some avocados were in the basket. 2 more avocados were added to the basket. Now there are 17 avocados. How many avocados were in the basket before more avocados were added?

ADDITION

33. **11 red apples and 3 green apples are in the basket. How many apples are in the basket?**

---

34. **2 balls are in the basket. 15 more balls are put in the basket. How many balls are in the basket now?**

---

35. **2 plums were in the basket. More plums were added to the basket. Now there are 6 plums. How many plums were added to the basket?**

---

36. **23 apricots were in the basket. 14 are red and the rest are green. How many apricots are green?**

ADDITION

37. **7 bananas were in the basket. More bananas were added to the basket. Now there are 10 bananas. How many bananas were added to the basket?**

38. **2 plums are in the basket. 11 more plums are put in the basket. How many plums are in the basket now?**

39. **Michele has 2 more apricots than Marcie. Marcie has 5 apricots. How many apricots does Michele have?**

40. **Jake has 14 pears and Billy has 10 pears. How many pears do Jake and Billy have together?**

SUBTRACTION

SUBTRACTION

41. 7 apricots are in the basket. 6 are red and the rest are green. How many apricots are green?

....

42. 9 oranges were in the basket. Some of the oranges were removed from the basket. Now there are 3 oranges. How many oranges were removed from the basket?

....

43. Billy has 5 apples. David has 6 apples. How many more apples does David have than Billy?

....

44. Marcie has 0 fewer pears than Jennifer. Jennifer has 3 pears. How many pears does Marcie have?

....

SUBTRACTION

45. Ellen has 0 fewer peaches than Jackie. Jackie has 9 peaches. How many peaches does Ellen have?

46. 7 pears are in the basket. 7 are red and the rest are green. How many pears are green?

47. Some apricots were in the basket. 5 apricots were taken from the basket. Now there are 0 apricots. How many apricots were in the basket before some of the apricots were taken?

48. 4 oranges were in the basket. Some of the oranges were removed from the basket. Now there is 1 orange. How many oranges were removed from the basket?

SUBTRACTION

49. 6 plums are in the basket. 5 are red and the rest are green. How many plums are green?

....

50. 8 apples were in the basket. Some of the apples were removed from the basket. Now there are 2 apples. How many apples were removed from the basket?

....

51. 5 balls are in the basket. 2 balls are taken out of the basket. How many balls are in the basket now?

....

52. Amy has 1 fewer avocado than Ellen. Ellen has 3 avocados. How many avocados does Amy have?

....

SUBTRACTION

53. 3 apples were in the basket. Some of the apples were removed from the basket. Now there are 0 apples. How many apples were removed from the basket?

54. 9 apricots are in the basket. 9 apricots are taken out of the basket. How many apricots are in the basket now?

55. Steven has 4 pears. Adam has 5 pears. How many more pears does Adam have than Steven?

56. Some oranges were in the basket. 2 oranges were taken from the basket. Now there are 2 oranges. How many oranges were in the basket before some of the oranges were taken?

SUBTRACTION

57. **7 balls were in the basket. Some of the balls were removed from the basket. Now there are 2 balls. How many balls were removed from the basket?**

58. **Some apples were in the basket. 4 apples were taken from the basket. Now there are 4 apples. How many apples were in the basket before some of the apples were taken?**

59. **Allan has 2 avocados. Adam has 4 avocados. How many more avocados does Adam have than Allan?**

60. **Janet has 1 fewer banana than Ellen. Ellen has 7 bananas. How many bananas does Janet have?**

SUBTRACTION

61. Marin has 0 fewer peaches than Jackie. Jackie has 6 peaches. How many peaches does Marin have?

62. 8 bananas are in the basket. 6 bananas are taken out of the basket. How many bananas are in the basket now?

63. Jake has 6 pears. Billy has 8 pears. How many more pears does Billy have than Jake?

64. 5 avocados were in the basket. Some of the avocados were removed from the basket. Now there are 3 avocados. How many avocados were removed from the basket?

SUBTRACTION

65. Some plums were in the basket. 7 plums were taken from the basket. Now there is 1 plum. How many plums were in the basket before some of the plums were taken?

66. 4 pears are in the basket. 2 are red and the rest are green. How many pears are green?

67. Jake has 7 peaches. Steven has 9 peaches. How many more peaches does Steven have than Jake?

68. 7 avocados were in the basket. Some of the avocados were removed from the basket. Now there are 0 avocados. How many avocados were removed from the basket?

SUBTRACTION

69. 13 apricots were in the basket. Some of the apricots were removed from the basket. Now there are 2 apricots. How many apricots were removed from the basket?

70. Some apples were in the basket. 2 apples were taken from the basket. Now there is 1 apple. How many apples were in the basket before some of the apples were taken?

71. Jackie has 3 fewer peaches than Amy. Amy has 15 peaches. How many peaches does Jackie have?

72. Adam has 12 avocados. Steven has 13 avocados. How many more avocados does Steven have than Adam?

SUBTRACTION

73. 9 plums were in the basket. Some of the plums were removed from the basket. Now there is 1 plum. How many plums were removed from the basket?

74. Jennifer has 5 fewer balls than Amy. Amy has 13 balls. How many balls does Jennifer have?

75. Brian has 4 apricots. Allan has 5 apricots. How many more apricots does Allan have than Brian?

76. Some marbles were in the basket. 2 marbles were taken from the basket. Now there are 0 marbles. How many marbles were in the basket before some of the marbles were taken?

SUBTRACTION

77. **15 balls are in the basket. 15 are red and the rest are green. How many balls are green?**

....

78. **Marcie has 0 fewer pears than Sharon. Sharon has 6 pears. How many pears does Marcie have?**

....

79. **12 apples are in the basket. 10 apples are taken out of the basket. How many apples are in the basket now?**

....

80. **7 apricots were in the basket. Some of the apricots were removed from the basket. Now there are 0 apricots. How many apricots were removed from the basket?**

....

ANSWERS

1. Jake has 7 pears and Brian has 9 pears. How many pears do Jake and Brian have together?

16

2. 3 apples were in the basket. More apples were added to the basket. Now there are 7 apples. How many apples were added to the basket?

4

3. 9 balls are in the basket. 10 more balls are put in the basket. How many balls are in the basket now?

19

4. Some peaches were in the basket. 5 more peaches were added to the basket. Now there are 15 peaches. How many peaches were in the basket before more peaches were added?

10

5. 2 pears were in the basket. More pears were added to the basket. Now there are 4 pears. How many pears were added to the basket?

2

6. 6 red marbles and 9 green marbles are in the basket. How many marbles are in the basket?

15

7. 15 balls were in the basket. 8 are red and the rest are green. How many balls are green?

7

8. Marcie has 7 more oranges than Marin. Marin has 8 oranges. How many oranges does Marcie have?

15

9. **Allan has 10 peaches and Donald has 4 peaches. How many peaches do Allan and Donald have together?**

14

10. **3 plums are in the basket. 2 more plums are put in the basket. How many plums are in the basket now?**

5

11. **6 marbles were in the basket. 3 are red and the rest are green. How many marbles are green?**

3

12. **Some balls were in the basket. 7 more balls were added to the basket. Now there are 17 balls. How many balls were in the basket before more balls were added?**

10

13. **Paul has 2 apples and Steven has 8 apples. How many apples do Paul and Steven have together?**

10

14. **Ellen has 2 more marbles than Sandra. Sandra has 8 marbles. How many marbles does Ellen have?**

10

15. **14 bananas were in the basket. 10 are red and the rest are green. How many bananas are green?**

4

16. **2 apricots were in the basket. More apricots were added to the basket. Now there are 4 apricots. How many apricots were added to the basket?**

2

17. 5 plums are in the basket. 6 more plums are put in the basket. How many plums are in the basket now?

11

18. Michele has 2 more bananas than Sandra. Sandra has 6 bananas. How many bananas does Michele have?

8

19. 7 pears were in the basket. 4 are red and the rest are green. How many pears are green?

3

20. 4 red apricots and 8 green apricots are in the basket. How many apricots are in the basket?

12

21. Some pears were in the basket. 9 more pears were added to the basket. Now there are 15 pears. How many pears were in the basket before more pears were added?

6

22. Marin has 13 more apricots than Sharon. Sharon has 12 apricots. How many apricots does Marin have?

25

23. Donald has 14 oranges and Adam has 6 oranges. How many oranges do Donald and Adam have together?

20

24. 14 balls were in the basket. 5 are red and the rest are green. How many balls are green?

9

25. 11 pears were in the basket. 6 are red and the rest are green. How many pears are green?

5

26. Donald has 14 balls and Paul has 12 balls. How many balls do Donald and Paul have together?

26

27. Some oranges were in the basket. 4 more oranges were added to the basket. Now there are 6 oranges. How many oranges were in the basket before more oranges were added?

2

28. 15 plums are in the basket. 3 more plums are put in the basket. How many plums are in the basket now?

18

29. 9 balls are in the basket. 11 more balls are put in the basket. How many balls are in the basket now?

20

30. 4 plums were in the basket. More plums were added to the basket. Now there are 15 plums. How many plums were added to the basket?

11

31. 17 apricots were in the basket. 3 are red and the rest are green. How many apricots are green?

14

32. Some avocados were in the basket. 2 more avocados were added to the basket. Now there are 17 avocados. How many avocados were in the basket before more avocados were added?

15

33. **11 red apples and 3 green apples are in the basket. How many apples are in the basket?**

14

34. **2 balls are in the basket. 15 more balls are put in the basket. How many balls are in the basket now?**

17

35. **2 plums were in the basket. More plums were added to the basket. Now there are 6 plums. How many plums were added to the basket?**

4

36. **23 apricots were in the basket. 14 are red and the rest are green. How many apricots are green?**

9

37. **7 bananas were in the basket. More bananas were added to the basket. Now there are 10 bananas. How many bananas were added to the basket?**

3

38. **2 plums are in the basket. 11 more plums are put in the basket. How many plums are in the basket now?**

13

39. **Michele has 2 more apricots than Marcie. Marcie has 5 apricots. How many apricots does Michele have?**

7

40. **Jake has 14 pears and Billy has 10 pears. How many pears do Jake and Billy have together?**

24

41. 7 apricots are in the basket. 6 are red and the rest are green. How many apricots are green?

1

42. 9 oranges were in the basket. Some of the oranges were removed from the basket. Now there are 3 oranges. How many oranges were removed from the basket?

6

43. Billy has 5 apples. David has 6 apples. How many more apples does David have than Billy?

1

44. Marcie has 0 fewer pears than Jennifer. Jennifer has 3 pears. How many pears does Marcie have?

3

45. Ellen has 0 fewer peaches than Jackie. Jackie has 9 peaches. How many peaches does Ellen have?

9

46. 7 pears are in the basket. 7 are red and the rest are green. How many pears are green?

0

47. Some apricots were in the basket. 5 apricots were taken from the basket. Now there are 0 apricots. How many apricots were in the basket before some of the apricots were taken?

5

48. 4 oranges were in the basket. Some of the oranges were removed from the basket. Now there is 1 orange. How many oranges were removed from the basket?

3

49. **6 plums are in the basket. 5 are red and the rest are green. How many plums are green?**

1

50. **8 apples were in the basket. Some of the apples were removed from the basket. Now there are 2 apples. How many apples were removed from the basket?**

6

51. **5 balls are in the basket. 2 balls are taken out of the basket. How many balls are in the basket now?**

3

52. **Amy has 1 fewer avocado than Ellen. Ellen has 3 avocados. How many avocados does Amy have?**

2

53. **3 apples were in the basket. Some of the apples were removed from the basket. Now there are 0 apples. How many apples were removed from the basket?**

3

54. **9 apricots are in the basket. 9 apricots are taken out of the basket. How many apricots are in the basket now?**

0

55. **Steven has 4 pears. Adam has 5 pears. How many more pears does Adam have than Steven?**

1

56. **Some oranges were in the basket. 2 oranges were taken from the basket. Now there are 2 oranges. How many oranges were in the basket before some of the oranges were taken?**

4

57. **7 balls were in the basket. Some of the balls were removed from the basket. Now there are 2 balls. How many balls were removed from the basket?**

5

58. **Some apples were in the basket. 4 apples were taken from the basket. Now there are 4 apples. How many apples were in the basket before some of the apples were taken?**

8

59. **Allan has 2 avocados. Adam has 4 avocados. How many more avocados does Adam have than Allan?**

2

60. **Janet has 1 fewer banana than Ellen. Ellen has 7 bananas. How many bananas does Janet have?**

6

61. **Marin has 0 fewer peaches than Jackie. Jackie has 6 peaches. How many peaches does Marin have?**

6

62. **8 bananas are in the basket. 6 bananas are taken out of the basket. How many bananas are in the basket now?**

2

63. **Jake has 6 pears. Billy has 8 pears. How many more pears does Billy have than Jake?**

2

64. **5 avocados were in the basket. Some of the avocados were removed from the basket. Now there are 3 avocados. How many avocados were removed from the basket?**

2

65. Some plums were in the basket. 7 plums were taken from the basket. Now there is 1 plum. How many plums were in the basket before some of the plums were taken?

8

66. 4 pears are in the basket. 2 are red and the rest are green. How many pears are green?

2

67. Jake has 7 peaches. Steven has 9 peaches. How many more peaches does Steven have than Jake?

2

68. 7 avocados were in the basket. Some of the avocados were removed from the basket. Now there are 0 avocados. How many avocados were removed from the basket?

7

69. 13 apricots were in the basket. Some of the apricots were removed from the basket. Now there are 2 apricots. How many apricots were removed from the basket?

11

70. Some apples were in the basket. 2 apples were taken from the basket. Now there is 1 apple. How many apples were in the basket before some of the apples were taken?

3

71. Jackie has 3 fewer peaches than Amy. Amy has 15 peaches. How many peaches does Jackie have?

12

72. Adam has 12 avocados. Steven has 13 avocados. How many more avocados does Steven have than Adam?

1

73. **9 plums were in the basket. Some of the plums were removed from the basket. Now there is 1 plum. How many plums were removed from the basket?**

8

74. **Jennifer has 5 fewer balls than Amy. Amy has 13 balls. How many balls does Jennifer have?**

8

75. **Brian has 4 apricots. Allan has 5 apricots. How many more apricots does Allan have than Brian?**

1

76. **Some marbles were in the basket. 2 marbles were taken from the basket. Now there are 0 marbles. How many marbles were in the basket before some of the marbles were taken?**

2

77. **15 balls are in the basket. 15 are red and the rest are green. How many balls are green?**

0

78. **Marcie has 0 fewer pears than Sharon. Sharon has 6 pears. How many pears does Marcie have?**

6

79. **12 apples are in the basket. 10 apples are taken out of the basket. How many apples are in the basket now?**

2

80. **7 apricots were in the basket. Some of the apricots were removed from the basket. Now there are 0 apricots. How many apricots were removed from the basket?**

7

Made in the USA
Las Vegas, NV
14 April 2025